My Legacy

A Book About

_____

(your name here)

Table of Contents

Introduction

"The trouble is, you think you have time."
- Buddha

Have you known anyone who has died unexpectedly? Most people who have died have done so without a will and without sharing their wishes regarding their funeral arrangements.   This leaves family members with many unanswered questions. Why does this happen? Most likely because they thought they had time....

This is a book about your life as well as your death. It's a memoir/a journal you can complete as you experience life and express your wishes regarding your death, as it is the only thing inevitable in life.

This book was designed for anyone, of just about any age, to fill out. It allows grieving family members, who are left behind after your passing, to know your after-death wishes. It provides them with answers to questions they might have and maybe most importantly, your hand-written words to cherish.

Sometimes it is difficult to have a discussion with loved ones about death and dying. My hope is that this book can help.

About Me

My full name _____

Where I was born_____

Where I grew up_____

My birthday _____

My hair color_____

My eye color_____

My height_____

My weight_____

My parents' names_____

_____

_____

_____

My siblings' names _____

_____

_____

_____

_____

_____

_____

My mother's maiden name_____

Family health history/concerns _____

_____

_____

_____

Where I live_____

Where I wish I lived_____

When I received and started working on this book _____

_____

_____

A Picture of Me

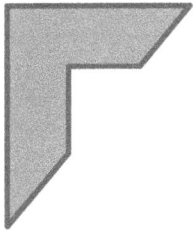

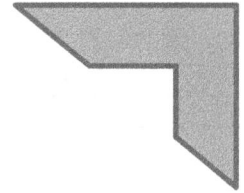

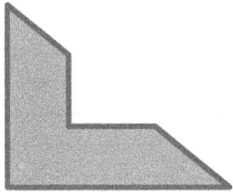

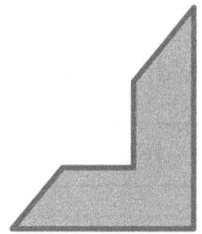

My Work Life

Where I work

_____

When I started my current job

_____

What my job entails

_____
_____
_____
_____
_____
_____

The best part about my job

_____
_____
_____
_____
_____
_____

The worst part about my job

_____
_____
_____
_____
_____
_____

My dream job would be

_____
_____
_____
_____

Jobs I have had

_____
_____
_____
_____
_____
_____
_____

My Spouse/My Partner

My spouse/partner's name
_____

When we first met
_____

Where we first met
_____

Our anniversary
_____

When we got engaged
_____

The proposal
_____
_____
_____
_____
_____
_____
_____
_____
_____
_____

Our wedding date
_____

Where we got married
_____

Who was in our wedding party
_____
_____
_____
_____
_____
_____
_____

Our favorite activities as a couple

_____
_____
_____
_____
_____
_____
_____
_____
_____

What I love most about my spouse/partner

_____
_____
_____
_____
_____
_____
_____
_____

Things we have in common

_____
_____
_____
_____
_____
_____
_____

Things we disagree on

_____
_____
_____
_____
_____
_____
_____
_____
_____

What makes us a great couple

_____
_____
_____
_____
_____

Pictures of My Spouse/Partner

Pictures of My Spouse/Partner

My Children

Child/Children's name(s) and birthday(s)

_____
_____
_____
_____
_____
_____
_____
_____

What I love most about being a parent

_____
_____
_____
_____
_____
_____

The most difficult part of being a parent

_____
_____
_____
_____
_____
_____

My wishes for my child(ren)

_____
_____
_____
_____
_____
_____
_____
_____
_____
_____
_____
_____
_____
_____

Pictures of My Children

Pictures of My Children

My Pets

Pet's name(s), breed(s) and birthday(s)

_____
_____
_____
_____
_____
_____
_____

My wishes for my pet(s) should something happen to me

_____
_____
_____
_____
_____
_____
_____
_____
_____

Veterinary contact information

_____
_____
_____

Other pertinent information (allergies, likes, dislikes, etc...)

_____
_____
_____
_____
_____
_____
_____
_____

My Bucket List

My Favorites

Favorite Colors

_____
_____

Favorite Foods

_____
_____
_____
_____

Favorite Drinks

_____
_____

Favorite Animals

_____
_____
_____

Favorite Sports Teams

_____
_____
_____
_____

Favorite Athletes

_____
_____
_____
_____

Favorite Songs

_____
_____
_____
_____
_____
_____

Favorite TV Shows

_____
_____
_____
_____

Favorite Sports to Play

_____

_____

_____

Favorite Sports to Watch

_____

_____

_____

Favorite Hobbies

_____

_____

_____

Favorite Restaurants

_____

_____

_____

_____

Favorite Season

_____

_____

Favorite Musicians/Bands

_____

_____

_____

_____

_____

Favorite Actors/Actresses

_____

_____

_____

Favorite Flowers/Plants

_____

_____

_____

Favorite Books

_____

_____

_____

_____

_____

Favorite Places to Shop

_____
_____
_____

Favorite Places to Go

_____
_____
_____

Favorite Quotes

_____
_____
_____
_____
_____
_____

Favorite Movies

_____
_____
_____
_____
_____

Favorite Sayings

_____
_____
_____
_____
_____

Favorite Places to Vacation

_____
_____
_____
_____

Other Favorites

_____
_____
_____
_____
_____
_____
_____

My Religious/Spiritual Beliefs

My Religious/Spiritual Affiliation

_____

Where I worship

_____

My Pastor/Priest/Spiritual Leader's name

_____

My favorite religious verses/spiritual quotes

_____
_____
_____
_____
_____
_____
_____
_____
_____
_____
_____
_____
_____
_____
_____
_____

My most memorable religious/spiritual experience(s)

_____
_____
_____
_____
_____
_____
_____
_____

My Family Tree

Great-Grandpa

Great-Grandpa

Great-Grandpa

Great-Grandpa

Great-Grandma

Great-Grandma

Great-Grandma

Great-Grandma

Grandpa

Grandpa

Grandma

Grandma

Dad

Mom

You

My Friends

My best friends

_____
_____
_____
_____
_____
_____

Things I like to do with my friends

_____
_____
_____
_____
_____
_____
_____
_____
_____
_____
_____

Some of my most memorable experiences with my friends

_____
_____
_____
_____
_____
_____
_____
_____
_____
_____
_____
_____
_____
_____
_____
_____
_____
_____

Pictures of Me, My Friends & Family

Pictures of Me, My Friends & Family

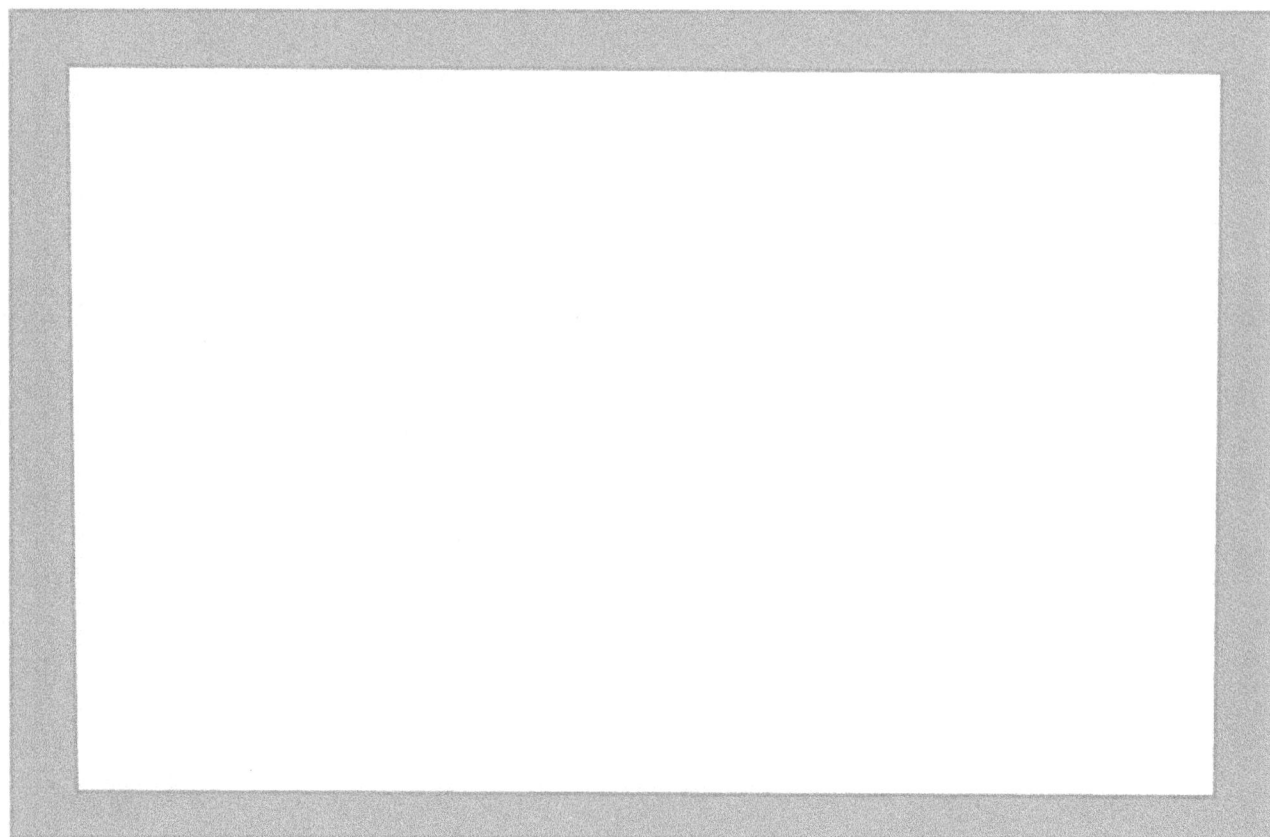

Pictures of Me, My Friends & Family

Growing Up

I lived ☐ in a house ☐ in an apartment ☐ on a farm ☐ (Other)_____

I lived with ☐ my parent(s) ☐ my grandparent(s) ☐ a foster family ☐ (other)_____

Where I went to elementary school_____

Where I went to jr. high school_____

Where I went to high school_____

Where I went to college_____

College degree(s)_____

Awards, certificates, designations

_____
_____
_____
_____

My military background

_____
_____
_____
_____
_____

My family heritage/background

_____
_____
_____
_____
_____

My first job was (where)_____, doing (what)_____
_____
_____

When I was a child I wanted to grow up to be

_____
_____
_____
_____

Growing up....

I played the following sport(s)

_____
_____
_____
_____
_____
_____

I played the following musical instrument(s)

_____
_____
_____
_____

Places I visited

_____
_____
_____
_____
_____
_____
_____

Who my childhood best friends were

_____
_____
_____
_____
_____

What I wish I would've done more

_____
_____
_____
_____
_____
_____

What I wish I would've done less

_____
_____
_____
_____
_____
_____
_____

Things I liked most about my childhood

_____
_____
_____
_____
_____
_____
_____
_____
_____
_____
_____
_____
_____
_____
_____
_____

Things I disliked most about my childhood

_____
_____
_____
_____
_____
_____
_____
_____
_____
_____
_____
_____

Family Traditions Included

My Life

Things I'm most proud of

☐ _____
☐ _____
☐ _____
☐ _____
☐ _____
☐ _____
☐ _____
☐ _____
☐ _____
☐ _____
☐ _____
☐ _____
☐ _____
☐ _____
☐ _____
☐ _____

Things I would have done differently

➤ _____
➤ _____
➤ _____
➤ _____
➤ _____
➤ _____
➤ _____
➤ _____
➤ _____
➤ _____
➤ _____
➤ _____
➤ _____
➤ _____
➤ _____
➤ _____

I want to be remembered as someone who was

- [ ] Fun
- [ ] Intelligent
- [ ] Witty
- [ ] Loyal
- [ ] Friendly
- [ ] Confident
- [ ] Happy
- [ ] Strong
- [ ] Supportive
- [ ] Controversial
- [ ] _____
- [ ] _____
- [ ] _____

- [ ] Caring
- [ ] Loving
- [ ] Funny
- [ ] Easy Going
- [ ] Passionate
- [ ] Determined
- [ ] Talented
- [ ] Adventurous
- [ ] Generous
- [ ] Helpful
- [ ] _____
- [ ] _____
- [ ] _____

- [ ] Athletic
- [ ] Faithful
- [ ] Sincere
- [ ] Thoughtful
- [ ] Understanding
- [ ] Modest
- [ ] Optimistic
- [ ] Independent
- [ ] Fearless
- [ ] Courageous
- [ ] _____
- [ ] _____
- [ ] _____

I think this is what happens when people pass away

- ☐ They go to heaven/hell
- ☐ They are reincarnated
- ☐ They become ghosts
- ☐ Nothing
- ☐ Other

What else do you believe?

_____
_____
_____
_____
_____
_____
_____
_____
_____
_____
_____
_____
_____
_____
_____
_____
_____
_____
_____

When I Die

I want my family/friends to know (my fears, desires, wishes, feelings)

_____
_____
_____
_____
_____
_____
_____
_____
_____
_____
_____
_____
_____
_____
_____
_____
_____
_____
_____
_____
_____
_____
_____
_____
_____
_____
_____
_____

After I Pass Away

I would like my family/friends to

☐ Have a wake/visitation

☐ Have my burial at a cemetery
   If buried, I want it to be at this cemetery
   _____

☐ Have a green burial (environmentally friendly) http://www.greenburials.org/

☐ Turn me into a tree https://urnabios.com/

☐ Cremate my body
   If cremated, I want the following done with my ashes
   _____
   _____
   _____

☐ I want to donate my body to science

☐ I want to donate my organs

☐ I have a Last Will and Testament
   (It is located_____)

☐ I have a Living Will
   (It is located_____)

I do not have a Last Will and Testament, but these are my wishes regarding my children/property/belongings

_____
_____
_____
_____
_____
_____
_____
_____
_____
_____
_____
_____
_____
_____
_____
_____
_____
_____
_____
_____
_____
_____
_____
_____
_____
_____
_____
_____
_____
_____
_____
_____

My Funeral

The funeral home where I would like my funeral to take place

_____

I would like the following flowers/plants/decorations

_____
_____

In my memory, I would like for donations to be made to the following charity/charities

_____
_____
_____

These are the songs I would like to have played

_____
_____
_____
_____
_____
_____
_____
_____

The outfit (or type of outfit) I would like to be buried/cremated in

_____
_____
_____

Other special requests

_____
_____
_____
_____
_____

How the Ideal Headstone Would Look

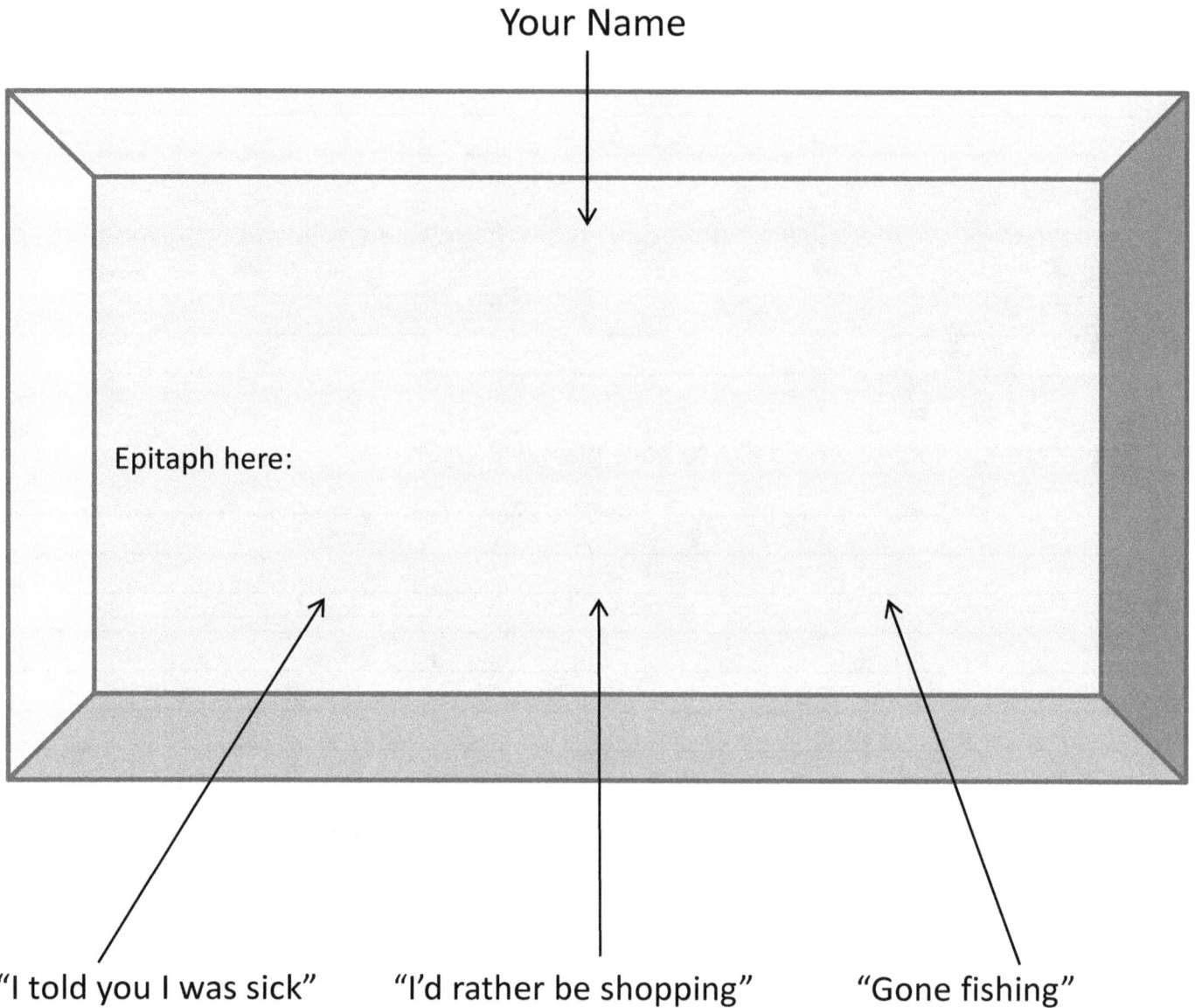

Your Name

Epitaph here:

"I told you I was sick"   "I'd rather be shopping"   "Gone fishing"

Other headstone specifications

_____

_____

_____

_____

If I were to write my own obituary it would go something like this

_____
_____
_____
_____
_____
_____
_____
_____
_____
_____
_____
_____
_____
_____
_____
_____
_____
_____
_____
_____
_____
_____
_____
_____
_____
_____
_____

Get help at www.obituaryguide.com

Get help at www.obituaryguide.com

Personal Information

Bank Account Info

Bank Name

_____

Account #s

_____

Bank Name

_____

Account #s

_____

Passwords

Email Address _____

Password _____

Email Address _____

Password_____

Facebook Account Login _____

Password_____

Twitter Account Login _____

Password_____

Other Social Media_____

Password_____

Life Insurance/Death Benefits Info

Life Insurance Company_____

Contact Information_____

Death Benefits_____

Contact Information_____

Investments/401K Info

Company Name_____

Website_____

Login_____

Password_____

Contact Info_____

Additional Personal Information

_____

_____

_____

_____

_____

_____

_____

_____

_____

_____

_____

_____

_____

_____

_____

_____

_____

_____

_____

_____

_____

_____

_____

_____

_____

_____

_____

Notes, Thoughts, Journal Entries

LETTERS TO FRIENDS/FAMILY

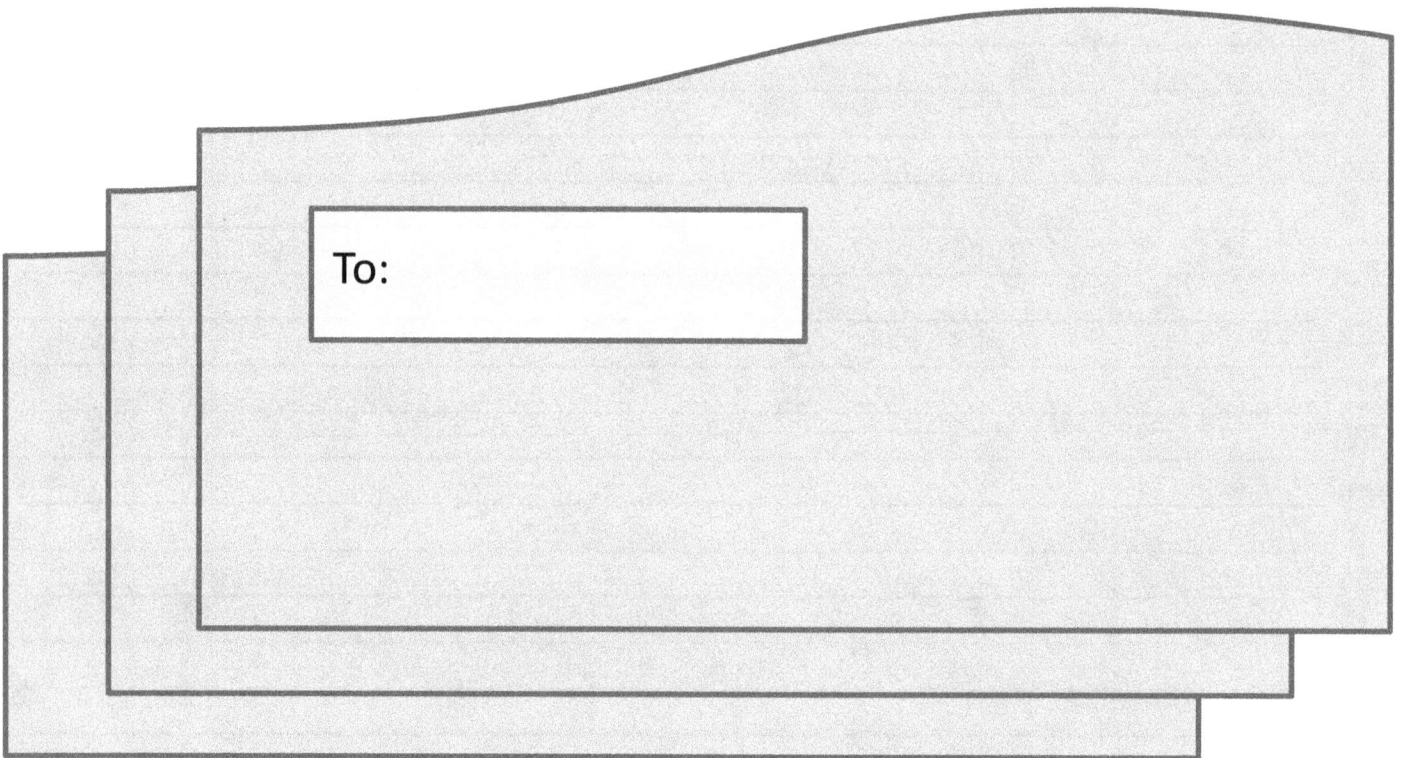

To:

Attach letters to your close friends and/or family members to this page
or put them in envelopes in the back of the book.

www.ingramcontent.com/pod-product-compliance
Lightning Source LLC
Chambersburg PA
CBHW081527040426
42447CB00013B/3366